Why There Is No God

The Essence of Richard Dawkins's "The God Delusion"

CURIOUS READER

Copyright © 2012 Curious Reader

All rights reserved.

ISBN: 1480150339
ISBN-13: 978-1480150331

CONTENTS

	Preface	i
1	Undeserved respect	1
2	What is the God Hypothesis?	5
3	How to argue that God exists	13
4	The ultimate argument against God's existence	21
5	How to explain religion	28
6	How to explain morality	36
7	The moral values of the Bible	41
8	The darker side of religion	48
9	Religion and children	53
10	Consolation and comfort	58
11	Highlights	63
	Notes from Curious Reader	67

PREFACE

Richard Dawkins's "The God Delusion" is an uncompromising critique of the religious worldview written by a preeminent evolutionary biologist and prominent social activist. This important book should not be ignored regardless of whether you are an avowed atheist or a diehard believer. However, many readers are put off by its long-winded style and multiple digressions, which are especially annoying when the author tries to settle some old scores with his numerous adversaries. This digest gives you the essence of Dawkins's book which is much easier to follow than the original. It contains all the important arguments and examples of "The God Delusion" without unnecessary verbiage and rhetorical figures. Although this is by no means a polemic against Dawkins's philosophical position, you can find some critical commentaries and additions at the end of the book.

1 UNDESERVED RESPECT

The central topic of this short chapter is the question of whether religions and religious believers deserve special respect of a kind that is usually not granted to other types of beliefs, such as political or moral ones. To what lengths should we go in order not to offend the followers of a particular religion? Is it right for a group of believers to demand high regard for their religious views and practices from people who don't share their faith? Before considering these questions, Dawkins draws some terminological distinctions and clarifies common misconceptions. One important distinction separates what Dawkins calls Einsteinian religion from supernatural religion. Einstein is known to have invoked the name of God several times in his writings (his most famous quotation of that kind is "God does not play dice"), and this fact is often exploited by religious people to promote their worldview. (They say something to the effect

"Look, even a mind as great as that of Einstein's acknowledges the necessity of postulating the existence of a Higher Being"). But Einstein himself made it perfectly clear that he did not believe in a personal God. His "religious" remarks only expressed his admiration of the beauty and harmony of the universe and its laws. Many scientists, among them Dawkins, admit that they have a quasi-mystical experience of transcendent wonder when contemplating nature and its beauty. But this does not mean that they are religious in the usual sense of the word.

To better clarify the difference between Einsteinian and supernatural religion, it may be useful to introduce the notions of theism, deism, and pantheism. Theists believe in the existence of a God who is a supernatural intelligence, and who is involved in our affairs, listens to our prayers, punishes our sins, etc. The followers of mainstream religions are typically theists. Deists, on the other hand, acknowledge that there is a supernatural being whom we call God, but believe that his only action relevant from our perspective was the creation of the universe. According to deism God is not interested in human affairs and does not intervene in them. For deists it does not make sense to worship God, since we cannot influence him in any way, and he does not care about our devotion to him. Finally, pantheism identifies God with the entire universe and its laws. The type of religion professed by Einstein and like-minded scientists is best interpreted as a version of pantheism, and not deism or theism.

Another ambiguous word which can cause confusion is the term "naturalism". In one sense of the word, naturalists are just those who study the natural world – scientists, biologists, physicists. But in philosophy naturalism is often contrasted with supernaturalism. Naturalists in this sense believe that there is nothing beyond the natural, physical world. They deny the existence of supernatural beings and miraculous occurrences defying natural laws. Naturalists maintain that human thoughts and emotions emerge from complex physical relations of the brain. Under this interpretation, naturalism comes very close to atheism.

Numerous examples can be given which illustrate the fact that religions and religious beliefs receive privileged treatment in media and politics. First of all, it is commonly thought that religious beliefs are especially vulnerable to offence, and therefore should be treated with the utmost respect. It is considered inappropriate to question somebody's religious views in the way we often criticize people's political choices and preferences. Another example of the preferential treatment enjoyed by religion in modern society is that the surest way to receive the status of a conscientious objector is to quote one's religious views which prevent one from fighting in a war. In contrast with that, giving moral or philosophical reasons is usually deemed insufficient for an objector to be exempted from military service. Religious leaders from different faith groups are always invited to participate in media discussions on important moral issues. Even the use of illegal hallucinogenic substances can be allowed if the claim is made that religious ceremonies require them.

The right to the freedom of religion is often given precedence over the freedom of speech. One particularly drastic example illustrating this fact is a recent scandal involving a Danish newspaper which published a series of cartoons depicting the prophet Muhammad. This caused massive protests and riots in Muslim countries, and calls were even made to assassinate the authors of the cartoons. Even so-called moderate Muslims condemned the publication of the cartoons, arguing that for the Muslims the person of the prophet Muhammad is sacred. But why should people who don't share the Muslim faith take this seriously? Why should respect be demanded even for the most fantastic beliefs, only because they are part of somebody's religious creed? In the conclusion of the first chapter Dawkins cautions the reader that while he has no intention to offend anybody, he will not shy away from stating bluntly his own negative views on religion.

2 WHAT IS THE GOD HYPOTHESIS?

In this chapter Dawkins makes general remarks about the meaning and status of the hypothesis that God exists. For the purpose of his analysis Dawkins expresses the God Hypothesis in the most defensible and charitable way which is not tied to any particular religious creed. As a starting point he formulates the God Hypothesis as stating that there is a supernatural, superhuman intelligent being who intentionally designed and created the entire universe.[1] It should be clear that such a broad hypothesis can be accepted not only by theists, but deists as well. However, later Dawkins adds to this characteristic the further assumption that God has not only created the universe but constantly maintains and supervises it, and that he can and does intervene in it by performing miracles and temporarily suspending the laws of nature. Thus the God Hypothesis under this reading becomes a statement which only a theist can fully embrace.

The God Hypothesis comes in many versions, depending on what particular set of religious beliefs we conjoin it with. Generally speaking, religions can be divided into polytheistic (admitting many divine beings) and monotheistic (accepting only one supreme being). Polytheistic religions had been widespread in the past, but they became gradually replaced with the monotheistic ones. The three monotheistic religions dominating the world today, known collectively as Abrahamic religions, are Judaism, Christianity, and Islam. However, there may be some doubts as to whether Christianity, especially Roman Catholicism, is truly a monotheistic faith. One controversial part of the Catholic teaching is the dogma of the Holy Trinity, i.e. the claim that there are three divine persons, the Father, the Son, and the Holy Spirit, that nevertheless constitute one God. The attempts of Christian theologians to reconcile the dogma of the Trinity with the assertion that there is only one God verge on accepting a logical contradiction. Moreover, the official Catholic doctrine admits that there are persons other than God himself who are worthy of worship and reverence: Virgin Mary, angels, and saints. It may be argued that for Catholics all these figures are divine in character, and therefore closely resemble lesser gods in polytheistic systems of beliefs.[2]

Deism is a watered-down version of monotheism, quite popular among philosophers and scientists of the age of Enlightenment. The deist God is a lofty figure, unconcerned with our affairs and indifferent to our prayers and pleas for forgiveness. He is the Great Designer of the universe, but once he had set it in motion he lost interest in it. The majority of the Founding Fathers of the American Republic were openly deists, if not outright atheists. This perhaps explains why one of the main pillars on which the newly created United States were based was secularism. Secularism meant that no faith was to be given the status of a preferred state religion. By insuring that no religion should be allowed to dominate the new Republic, the Founding Fathers wanted to avoid bloody religious conflicts like the ones which had beset England. Paradoxically, however, the secularism built into the foundations of the US might have contributed to the explosion of today's rampant religious movements across America. This is so, because various religious groups and churches freely compete with one another, and they use aggressive marketing techniques to acquire new converts. On the other hand, in the absence of strong competition the state-backed Church of England has slowly degenerated into little more than a social club.

Regardless of the political and social implications of one's religious beliefs, the key question remains: how much credence should we give to the God Hypothesis? Before thoroughly considering the main arguments for and against this hypothesis in the next two chapters, we can lay down the spectrum of possibilities regarding our evaluation of the God Hypothesis. At the extreme ends of the spectrum lie two opposing views: strong theism (the probability that the God Hypothesis is true is 100%) and strong atheism (the probability that God exists is 0%). But there are several possible intermediate views which assign to the God Hypothesis the probability greater than 0 but smaller than 100 percent. Right in the middle of the spectrum lies the position according to which the hypothesis that God exists and its negation are equally probable. This view is commonly known as (completely impartial) agnosticism. Agnostics generally admit that we don't have sufficient evidence to decide the God Hypothesis either way. Even though agnostics often draw scorn from both theists and atheists for apparently lacking backbone to take a firm stand on the issue, it has to be admitted that in many cases agnosticism is the only rational and scientifically responsible position. Such is the case for instance with the question of whether there is life outside of our planet, given the currently available evidence. But Dawkins's position on religious agnosticism is that it is unnecessarily defensive, because there are positive arguments showing that the God Hypothesis is actually much less probable than 50%.

Two main types of agnosticism can be distinguished: Temporary Agnosticism in Practice (TAP) and Permanent Agnosticism in Principle (PAP). TAP with respect to a particular hypothesis is a position according to which the considered hypothesis is either true or false, but at this particular moment we don't have enough evidence to decide which is the case. However, things may change in the future, as new evidence is discovered. On the other hand, PAP insists that there is no way to know even in principle whether the hypothesis of interest to us is true or false. An example of a hypothesis to which PAP is clearly applicable is the philosophical statement that all people have exactly the same impression when they see red (or any other color). As there is no way to get access to someone else's perceptions, such a hypothesis will forever remain in the realm of speculation.[3] Agnostics towards God's existence are usually of the second kind, claiming that this issue is strictly beyond our reach. But Dawkins argues that PAP does not imply that God's existence and non-existence are equiprobable. Even if the God hypothesis can never be conclusively verified or falsified, this does not mean that the statement itself is as probable as its negation.

To illustrate this point, Dawkins uses the famous teapot example invented by the philosopher Bertrand Russell. Let's consider the hypothesis that somewhere in space between the Earth and Mars there is a china teapot revolving around the Sun. The teapot is so small that even the most powerful telescopes on Earth can't reveal its existence. While we may be justified in adopting a PAP stance towards the existence of the teapot,[4] this does not imply that the probability of its existence should be estimated to be 50%. It is clear that without any additional reasons to believe that such a teapot should exist, the Teapot Hypothesis ought to be considered preposterous.[5] The teapot example illustrates the general rule which may be called "the burden of proof principle". The fictional proponents of the Teapot Hypothesis have the obligation to give positive arguments in favor of their stance (the burden of proof is on their side). It is not appropriate for them to declare that because their opponents can't disprove their claim, the hypothesis and its negation are equally probable.[6]

The assertion that God's existence can't be disproved is often associated with yet another controversial but widespread claim – the claim that science is irrevocably separated from religion. Dawkins uses the acronym NOMA (non-overlapping magisteria), coined by S.J. Gould, to refer to this position, held by many scientists and theologians alike. According to this popular view, science is simply incapable of evaluating the claim that God exists and supervises the world. Science deals with empirical, observable and measurable phenomena, while religion goes beyond these limitations to the realm of ultimate purposes and explanations, and also to the realm of morality. Another concise way to express this difference is by saying that science is concerned with *how* questions, whereas theology is prepared to answer *why* questions. But there are fundamental problems with this view. Even if we agree that there are certain ultimate questions which are beyond science's reach, there is no reason to believe that theology can answer them. Theology has a dubious reputation, and it is unclear what particular expertise it can bring to the table. Furthermore, the existence of mutually incompatible moral rules and values based on different religious beliefs makes it virtually impossible to found morality on theology.

But the main problem with NOMA is that it is most certainly false, given how the God Hypothesis is construed by mainstream religions. Theists of all stripes agree that God can (and does) perform miracles in the natural world – he can create matter out of nothing, he can make objects move in violation of all known laws, and so on. This means that a world with such a God would be a different place than a world without an omnipotent creator and overseer. And this difference can be in principle studied by science. Miraculous occurrences, such as raising people from the dead, being taken to heaven with the whole body, changing water into wine, involve physical, tangible objects, and definitely come within the purview of empirical science. Perhaps the deistic version of the God Hypothesis could lend some credence to NOMA, as in that case God is not assumed to create any events which would contradict the natural order of the universe. But even in this scenario it remains true that a universe created by a supernatural entity is a different place than a universe governed entirely by natural laws, and there is no reason why science should not be in principle capable of detecting this difference.

One example illustrating how science can evaluate religious claims is the so-called Great Prayer Experiment. The study, funded by the Templeton Foundation, was supposed to reveal whether prayers offered for sick people can actually speed up their recovery. 1,802 patients from six hospitals who had received coronary bypass surgery were selected to participate in the study. Each patient was assigned to one of three groups. One group received prayers from three church congregations, of which the patients were not informed. The second group did not receive any prayers, and similarly they did not know about that. The third group of patients received prayers and they were informed about this fact. The study did not reveal any statistically significant difference in the recovery time and the number of complications between the first and the second groups; however, the third group had a significantly higher number of complications (contradicting a possible suggestion that a placebo effect may be involved). The results of the Great Prayer Experiment are often dismissed on the basis of the fact that God doesn't answer prayers which were not given for a good reason. However, if the outcome of the study had been positive, this would definitely have been hailed in religious circles as a confirmation of God's direct intervention. Thus religious beliefs are testable by science.

3 HOW TO ARGUE THAT GOD EXISTS

Throughout history numerous arguments have been proposed in support of the God Hypothesis in one form or another. This chapter discusses a hodge-podge of some of the best-known of these arguments, and it closes with a brief analysis of a recent argument proposed in 2003 by Stephen Unwin. As it turns out, none of these multiple attempts stand up to careful scrutiny. To begin with, Saint Thomas Aquinas, the founding father of the official Catholic doctrine, formulated five arguments for God's existence, known as the five ways. All five of the proofs codified by St Thomas belong to the category of a posteriori arguments, because they use some premises derived from experience. The first three arguments rely on the denial of the idea of an infinite regress, that is a process or sequence which continues without end. The Unmoved Mover argument observes that every moving object has to be moved by something else, which also moves, but because this sequence cannot go on forever, there must be a first mover, and this mover is God. The Uncaused Cause argument has a similar structure, except that instead of objects moving other objects we talk now about things that cause other things. Again, God is postulated as the ultimate cause of everything in order to avoid a regress.

Dawkins calls Aquinas's third argument Cosmological, but it is also commonly referred to as the Argument from Contingency. It alleges that because all things in the universe are contingent, i.e. they might not have existed, there must have been a time when nothing existed at all. But in that case nothing would come into existence at all, since nothingness cannot produce anything. Thus there must be at least one necessary, non-contingent being. Further Aquinas explains that among all necessary beings one must be such that it owes its necessity to itself and nothing else (again, to avoid a regress), and this necessary being is identified with God. The fourth argument (the Argument from Degree) starts with the assumption that many properties, such as goodness, beauty or perfection, come in degrees. This means that some things can be better and some worse, some more beautiful and some less. But St Thomas Aquinas insists that things can be compared with one another with respect to those properties only if there exists a being that possesses all of them in the maximal degree (i.e. is the best, most beautiful and most perfect). And such a being is predictably identified with God.

Aquinas's fifth way deserves special attention, and Dawkins defers its proper analysis until the next chapter. This proof is known as the Teleological Argument, or the Argument from Design. It essentially states that some inanimate objects act as if for a purpose, but because they have no mind of their own, they must have been designed by someone who had this purpose in mind. Today virtually no one takes Aquinas's five arguments seriously, and they usually serve as study cases for philosophy students who learn how to identify logical fallacies in arguments. One of the key problems with St Thomas's proofs is that even if they prove the existence of some entity (which in itself is doubtful), this entity is not shown to be identical with God as we usually define him. How can we argue that the ultimate cause of everything in the universe (or the unmoved mover, or the being that possesses all properties in the maximal degree) answers our prayers and judges us after our death? For all we know the big bang could be identified as the first cause or the unmoved mover, but people don't go to churches, synagogues, or mosques to worship the big bang.[7]

The next philosophical argument considered by Dawkins belongs to the category of a priori arguments, because it does not rely on any premise derived from experience. It is known as the Ontological Argument, and was originally formulated by a forerunner of St Thomas Aquinas, St Anselm of Canterbury. Anselm notes that even an atheist should agree that God is defined as the only being such that nothing greater than him can be conceived. But if God didn't exist, then surely we could imagine an even greater being – namely a

God that exists. God's non-existence can't be reconciled with his definition, and therefore God has to exist. It is rather odd that such an important truth about the universe – that there is a God – could be derived from a mere definition, or a word game. Moreover, as Anselm's contemporary Gaunilo has shown, the same argument could be used to prove that virtually anything exists (Gaunilo used the example of the most perfect island which has to exist, otherwise it would not be the most perfect). Other critics, including philosophers David Hume and Immanuel Kant, identified the assumption that existence is more perfect than non-existence as the most controversial point of Anselm's reasoning.[8]

The next four arguments considered by Dawkins are less logical and more persuasive in character, aiming at shaking up the non-believer rather than establishing the validity of the conclusion beyond reasonable doubt. The Argument from Beauty insists that without the God Hypothesis it is hard to account for the sublime aesthetic values of the greatest works of art: music, poetry, paintings. There is no denying that innumerable artworks have been directly inspired by religion, from Michelangelo's paintings in the Sistine Chapel to Bach's oratorios. But this doesn't mean that these works could not have been created if the God Hypothesis were false. The Argument from Personal Experience relies on the fact that many people claim to have had strong religious experiences of various kinds, including direct visions of God himself. But we know that our brain is capable of creating visions and perceptions that do not correspond to reality.

One example is the optical illusion involving a rotating hollow mask, which is always seen by us as sticking out. To make sense of this perception, when the mask's hollow side is turned toward us, the brain interprets it as rotating in the opposite direction. The brain does not passively register sensory data, but actively creates a model of reality based on the data. This explains why people often report that they can see the faces of Jesus or Virgin Mary in apparently random patterns created by ordinary objects. Hallucinations and dreams can also explain alleged religious experiences. As Hume pointed out, a report of an apparent miraculous occurrence can justify a general hypothesis only if the falsity of this report would be more improbable than the hypothesis itself. But the explanation that a particular vision was caused by an illusion or a hallucination is much more likely than the God Hypothesis, therefore reports of religious experiences can do very little to support the claim that God exists.

One common way to argue for religion is to quote the authority of the holy texts – the Bible in the case of Christianity. But people who take the written words of Scripture at face value should first ask themselves what reasons, independent from their religious beliefs, do they have to trust this source. The authorship and the historical circumstances in which the writing took place have to be critically evaluated. In the case of the Bible it is common knowledge that many accounts in it have been doctored to serve particular purposes. For instance, the story of the birth of Jesus, including the choice of his birthplace in Bethlehem, was embellished to make it fit the prophecies from the Old Testament. There are various historical inaccuracies and numerous contradictions in the four gospels. For example, Matthew traces Joseph's descent from king David via 28 generations, while Luke mentions 41 generations, and the names on the two lists don't even overlap. On top of the four official gospels which are included in the New Testament, there are other, so-called apocryphal accounts of the life and teaching of Jesus of Nazareth. They were excluded from the accepted version of the Bible by early Church authorities, probably because they contained even more embarrassing inaccuracies and fabrications.

Another way in which believers try to checkmate their opponents is by appealing to the authority of preeminent scientists. Virtually all great scientists of the past, including Newton, Galileo, and Kepler, were religious people. But this began to change, especially after Darwin. In the nineteenth century the number of deeply religious scientists was still high, including Michael Faraday, James Clerk Maxwell, and Lord Kelvin. However, the twentieth century saw a radical reversal of this trend. According to a poll conducted in 1998 in the USA, only about 7 percent of the members of the National Academy of Science profess a belief in a personal God. A similar study carried out in Great Britain revealed that only 3.3 percent of the Fellows of the Royal Academy of Science agree strongly with the statement that a personal God exists. Yet another study found a strong negative correlation between religiosity and education in the US. Apart from the fact that generally arguments from authority carry little if any logical weight, the argument from religious scientists is clearly based on a false premise.

An original attempt to convince the non-believer was made by the great French mathematician and philosopher Blaise Pascal. Pascal considered the choice between believing and non-believing not as a theoretical issue, but a practical one. His question was not who is right, but whose decision is more rational. He argued that believing in God is much more rational regardless of the probability of the God Hypothesis, because if we turn out to be right, we will win a great prize, whereas if we are wrong, the loss is minimal. However, for the non-believer the situation is opposite: the loss is potentially huge (eternal damnation) while the win rather meager. Thus we should opt for religion. This argument has been criticized for not taking into account that it may be psychologically impossible to force oneself into believing something purely because it is useful. Also, the argument assumes that God will reward anybody who believes in him for whatever reason, but what if he actually punishes those who choose religion purely for ulterior motives? Pascal also ignores the fact that the alternative to the existence of the Christian God may be not merely his non-existence, but the existence of a different type of god who is jealous and vengeful. In this case the entire calculus of wins and losses collapses, as it is no longer true that the believer in the Christian God doesn't risk much.

Stephen Unwin has recently put forward an argument for God's existence based on Bayes's Theorem. This simple theorem of the probability calculus tells us how to adjust the probability of a given hypothesis in light of new evidence, given that we know how probable the evidence is under the assumption that the hypothesis is true, and how probable it is when the hypothesis is assumed to be false.[9] Unwin starts his argument with complete uncertainty, assigning to the God hypothesis and its negation equal chances. Then he considers six factors bearing on the hypothesis, such as the fact that we have a sense of goodness, the existence of minor miracles, the existence of major miracles, the existence of religious experiences, and also the fact that there is evil in the world. After assigning numerical likelihoods to these factors and applying Bayes's Theorem, he comes up with the result that the probability of God's existence should be estimated at 67 percent. The main problem with this argument is that the choice of the six factors and their numerical weighting seems to be completely arbitrary. Dawkins also disagrees with Unwin's assumption that the existence of evil lessens the likelihood of the existence of God. The problem of evil is usually seen as a challenge to theology (known as the problem of theodicy). However, the God Hypothesis as defined by Dawkins does not include the assumption that God is benevolent, and therefore the argument from evil does not apply to it.

4 THE ULTIMATE ARGUMENT AGAINST GOD'S EXISTENCE

This is the central chapter of the entire book, as it contains Dawkins's main argument against the God Hypothesis. The argument, dubbed by him The Ultimate Boeing 747 Gambit, is actually a reversed variant of the popular theistic argument from improbability (which, in turn, can be traced back to St Thomas's Argument from Design). Theists often point out that the complex forms of life existing on Earth could not have been produced by natural, random processes – the likelihood of such an occurrence is comparable to the chance of a hurricane creating a fully functioning Boeing 747 out of bits and pieces from a junkyard. Later in the chapter Dawkins explains step by step that this argument is based on a gross misinterpretation of the way evolution works (it is by no means a random process), but his quick and decisive rebuttal of the improbability argument is that it does not help the theists in the least. Their answer to the improbability problem is that God must have designed and created all the "irreducibly complex" forms of life on our planet. But the theists overlook the fact that the creator of such improbable things must himself be extremely improbable. God is the "Ultimate Boeing 747", as his existence is an even greater enigma than the existence of all complex structures in the natural world. To put it briefly, the question is: if God designed the world, who designed God? The God Hypothesis does not solve the problem of improbability but only moves it one step further to a higher level.[10]

The argument from improbability is based on the mistaken assumption that there are only two ways living creatures can come into being: either by design or by chance. But in fact there is a third alternative – natural selection – which is by no means chancy. Natural selection is a cumulative process consisting of a large number of only slightly improbable events, which together can create a very improbable outcome over a long period of time. Dawkins uses the metaphor of Mount Improbable to explain this phenomenon. A mountain which has a sheer cliff on one side may look impossible to climb, but on the other side there may be a long, gentle slope leading to the summit. Jumping up the steep cliff may indeed look like an extremely lucky coincidence, but evolution works its way slowly up the gentle side of the mountain.

One reason why theists (or creationists) commit the error of ignoring the existence of a third option besides design and chance is their too strong interpretation of the "irreducible complexity" of living organisms. A biological unit is called irreducibly complex if the removal of even one of its parts causes it to stop functioning. This conception assumes that the functioning of a given organ is an all-or-nothing matter – either it functions or it doesn't – and therefore it must have been designed as a complete unit. But in fact we know that many organs can still perform some of their functions even when slightly damaged or underdeveloped. Virtually all animals are equipped with eyes, but some of them are very rudimentary, capable of detecting only shades and light, but no images. Such a primitive eye is, in a sense, less than half of the human eye; nevertheless it is still useful from an evolutionary perspective, because it enables the animal to escape from a predator or detect prey. Primitive wings may not be sufficient for long-distance flights, but they can still be helpful when jumping from tree to tree. These facts illustrate how it is possible for evolution to develop amazingly complex organs by gradual improvements on the already existing features.

Creationists use the notion of irreducible complexity each time when they are unable to find a scientific explanation of a given phenomenon. This method of argumentation is known as the God of the gaps strategy, where God is invoked any time an unsolved problem is encountered. But this is not the way science works. Unsolved problems are things that science thrives on, because they create a challenge and motivate future investigations. On the other hand, explaining away a particular troublesome phenomenon by postulating God's intervention fosters complacency and does not stimulate further research. The gap strategy is also very weak, because it is based on our ignorance, which is gradually eliminated by the advances of scientific understanding. Sometimes gaps in scientific knowledge which supposedly support divine intervention are exaggerated or distorted by creationists. One particular example of such a situation is the standard creationist argument against evolution using the fact that there are some gaps in the fossil records. This argument doesn't take into account that the fossilization of dead animals is an extremely rare process occurring only under special conditions, and therefore we should expect to have missing transition forms between subsequent stages of development in the fossil records.

Evolution explains the development of an incredible variety of life forms with the help of natural selection. But the emergence of life itself can't be explained in that way, since before life appeared on our planet there had been no biological evolution to begin with. Hence some theists pin their hopes on the origin of life, which was certainly an extremely improbable occurrence. But because it was a unique event, it can be actually scientifically explained with the help of the so-called anthropic principle. Two versions of the anthropic principle can be distinguished: planetary and cosmological. The planetary version of the anthropic argument can be illustrated with the help of the following example. We know that the Earth satisfies the very strict conditions necessary for life to occur. Earth's location relative to the Sun (within the so-called Goldilocks zone: not too hot, not too cold) makes it possible for liquid water to form. The Moon stabilizes our planet, preventing it from wobbling wildly and thus allowing it to maintain regular seasons. The gravitational pull of Jupiter protects us from cosmic debris which could collide with the Earth and kill off all its life. But the question can be asked: why is our planet so amazingly accurately attuned to hosting life? One obvious reply is that it was designed to serve this purpose, but this leaves us with the question "Who designed the designer?". But an alternative, offered by the anthropic approach, is simply that the conditions on Earth had to be right, otherwise we wouldn't be here now, discussing this issue. The anthropic principle explains the marvelous coincidence enabling Earth to sustain life by the fact that we are present here.[11]

A similar approach can be adopted to the problem of the origin of life. Liquid water is necessary for life, but is far from sufficient. Life starts when elements required for reproduction and heredity are present: either DNA or the related molecule RNA. Once these elements are in place, natural selection can start working its magic. But the spontaneous creation of a molecule responsible for heredity seems to be highly improbable, and so far no one has succeeded in creating life artificially in a lab. Again, two explanations of why life indeed began on our planet against all odds are available: the design explanation and the anthropic one. The anthropic explanation is that had life not begun on Earth, we wouldn't be around to ask the question in the first place. Moreover, it may be observed that the anthropic explanation in this case is of a statistical type. We can estimate that the number of planets in the universe is so enormous that even if we eliminate the vast majority of them which could not possibly support life, still the number of potentially life-bearing planets is incredibly huge. By the laws of statistics, then, some of them are expected to actually harbor life. And we don't have to look for the tiny number of the lucky ones in the vast expanses of the universe, for we are on one of them not by luck but by necessity.

The cosmological version of the anthropic principle of explanation, in turn, addresses a similar question with respect to the whole universe. Science tells us that if the laws of nature had been slightly different from what they actually are, life as we know it would never have arisen. Physicists list six fundamental constants governing the basic interactions of matter. One of them for instance characterizes the so-called strong forces between the components of the nucleus. If this number was only slightly lower or higher, there would be only hydrogen atoms, or no hydrogen atoms at all in the universe, and no interesting chemistry would be possible. Theists use facts like these to argue that God must have personally fine-tuned all six parameters to make this universe an inhabitable place. The anthropic principle, on the other hand, simply explains this incredible coincidence by the fact that without it we wouldn't be able to ask for any explanation, because we wouldn't be here. But there is one important difference between the planetary and the cosmological versions of the anthropic principle. In the cosmological version we can't appeal to statistical reasoning because there is only one universe. To avoid this problem a multiverse theory has been proposed. It assumes that there is actually a myriad of different universes to which our universe belongs. These universes may be either parallel (existing "simultaneously" with our one) or serial (after our universe vanishes in a big crunch, a new one will appear, and so on). Each universe has a different set of laws, and we occupy one of those whose laws allow for the creation and development of organic life. This is obviously not a coincidence, as we ourselves are examples of organic life.

It has to be stressed that even though the statistical argument of the anthropic kind can explain a one-off even such as the origin of life, it can never explain the countless numbers of biological adaptations appearing on Earth. For that we need a new mechanism: the generalized process for optimizing biological species we call natural selection. And no divine intervention can help us either, for we can always repeat the same question with respect to the Designer. To satisfactorily explain the existence of the vast number of biological organisms we need Darwin's crane, not theists' skyhook.

5 HOW TO EXPLAIN RELIGION

What scientific explanation can we offer for the fact that religion is so commonplace in virtually all societies? Dawkins considers this question in the framework of the Darwinian theory of evolution. Seen from this perspective, religious practices and rituals seem utterly mysterious. They consume vast amounts of time and energy without bringing any obvious benefits in terms of survival or reproduction. Religious beliefs may even put their followers in danger by making them risk their lives. Because natural selection tends to eliminate wasteful and unproductive types of behavior, not to mention ones that endanger our survival, it is a challenge to explain why religions flourish in all known cultures. One possible strategy to solve this puzzle is to try to find direct advantages of religion. There is evidence indicating that religious beliefs may protect some people from stress-related diseases. But this fact can hardly explain the worldwide pervasiveness of religion. Similar psychological explanations point at the fact that religious beliefs satisfy our curiosity or provide consolation and comfort. However, these are at best proximate, not ultimate explanations of the existence of religion. For a Darwinian, an ultimate explanation of a given behavior must contain reference to the purpose it serves, which in turn can explain why natural selection favors it. For instance, an explanation of religious behavior in terms of the hyperactivity of a particular part of the brain would be a proximate one. To give an ultimate explanation we would have to explain the evolutionary purpose of this hypothetical neurological phenomenon.

Some alleged ultimate explanations of religion are given within the framework of the controversial group selection theory. This theory suggests that natural selection chooses not only among individuals, but among species or other groups of individuals. Religious beliefs or a particular kind may be seen as beneficial for the whole group – because they foster cooperation and altruism among its members, or because they prepare them to fight with other rival tribes. But the main problem with this theory is that low-level selection seems to be stronger than group selection. Those members of a given group who are slightly less altruistic than the others have a better chance of survival, and therefore the tendency to self-sacrifice for the good of the whole community will decline in future generations.

Dawkins's preferred explanation of religion is that it is a byproduct of some other characteristics which turned out to be beneficial for survival. It has to be noted first that not all features of living organisms which are favored by natural selection are themselves beneficial. Sometimes they simply result from other traits which proved to be helpful in the struggle for survival. This can be illustrated with the help of the following example. It is well known that moths have the unfortunate habit of flying straight into the candle flame. How can this suicidal behavior be preferred by natural selection? One possible explanation is that it is a byproduct of a method of navigation used by moths long before the appearance of artificial sources of light. Using only the light from the stars and the moon, moths learned how to maintain a steady course by keeping a constant angle between the light rays and the direction of their flight. This works well for sources of light which are at a considerable distance, so that the rays of light coming from them are almost parallel, but next to a candle or a street lamp the trajectory plotted in such a way will inevitably take a moth on a spiral path to the source of light. Still, on average the strategy works, so moths are unlikely to change their habit in the foreseeable future. It is possible that religion is a similar accidental byproduct of some useful adaptation. But the question is: what is this peculiar adaptation which leads to the proliferation of religious cults in human societies?

Dawkins's own favorite hypothesis is that the adaptation which is responsible for religious beliefs is the unconditional obedience of children to their parents. There are so many things critical for survival which children have to learn that they cannot merely rely on individual experience – learning by trial and error would be too protracted and too dangerous. The easiest way to pass on the cumulative wisdom of many generations is from parent to child, but this requires complete trust and uncritical acceptance of everything that the parents tell their children, including the rules regarding religious practices and beliefs. But Dawkins himself admits that the "gullible child" hypothesis does not explain why this and not that irrational belief takes hold in a community. It only ensures that beliefs which are already present will be perpetuated. Other explanations are more specific with respect to the particular kinds of religious beliefs as we know them. These explanations are developed within the growing field of evolutionary psychology. One of the fundamental assumptions of evolutionary psychology is that the brain can be separated into modules, each of which deals with a set of specialist needs. Religion can be seen as a byproduct of the functioning of several of these modules.

One suggestion along these lines is that the roots of religion lie in our instinctive dualism and teleology. Dualism is the philosophical position according to which there are two types of substances: material and spiritual. According to this stance, humans consist of matter and mind (or soul). Teleology, on the other hand, attributes purpose to inanimate objects and natural phenomena. Children for instance easily accept statements of the sort "Rains are for flowers to have water" which stress the teleological aspect of reality. The belief that souls exist and that the world has a purpose leads naturally to a religious standpoint. But why are dualism and teleology beneficial from an evolutionary perspective? This can be explained by the fact that when we have to make a quick decision on which our survival depends, we often take shortcuts. One such shortcut is called intentional stance, and it consists in an instinctive attribution of agency and intentions to entities around us, whether wild animals or inanimate objects that can potentially threaten us (boulders rolling downhill in an avalanche or falling trees). Intentional stance seems to be closely connected with dualism and teleology. Another possible psychological explanation of religion stresses the fact that we are primed by evolution to monogamous relations in order to raise children, and this in turn explains the phenomenon of romantic love as creating the strongest bonds. And religious faith has much in common with falling in love. The emotional relation with God is often described by believers in terms of deep, overwhelming love. Thus falling in love with God or Virgin Mary may be actually a byproduct of our evolutionarily beneficial propensity to create strong bonds with a member of the opposite sex.

Yet another potential explanation of religion is worth mentioning because it can also explain the persistence of other irrational beliefs (superstitions, racial prejudices, political sympathies, etc.). Some biologists suggest that there is an evolutionary mechanism guarding us against changing our mind too often, and therefore promoting sticking to one's established beliefs even in light of negative evidence. This behavior, referred to as "irrational persistence" is often connected with the mechanism of self-deception and wishful thinking. The similarities between these factors and religious thinking are hard to miss.

The creation and evolution of different systems of religious beliefs may be described within so-called memetic theory, which is a generalization of the Darwinian conception of natural selection. Natural selection in its most general form acts on alternative replicators. A replicator is any piece of information which makes near perfect copies of itself. Replicators that are good at copying themselves become more numerous. The standard example of a replicator is a gene, which is a fragment of DNA. But some biologists suggest that there may be other replicators not exemplified directly by physical objects. Such replicators may be for instance memes – units of cultural inheritance. Genes are known to compete with one another within a given pool. This competition is not direct but by proxy, that is by phenotypic traits of organisms. The same may be true of memes. One example of a meme can be a particular skill which is passed on from master to student. Skills that consist of a series of discrete operations, such as making an origami, can be transferred without significant loss of quality (they are self-normalizing). On the other hand, "analogue" skills, such as drawing, display a substantial degree of deterioration after several generations.

It is well known that genes do not act independently from each other. They are connected not only by physical links within chromosomes, but more importantly they collaborate with each other to create particular features of an organism. Some genes are successful only in the presence of other genes in that they jointly give rise to a beneficial trait. For instance, genes that program prey-detecting sense organs are successful within carnivore gene pools, but they would not be favored in herbivore gene pools. A similar phenomenon is postulated with respect to memes. Memes create groups called memeplexes. Memes within a particular memeplex are successful, but they need not be such outside of it.

According to the memetic theory of religion, religious ideas can be interpreted as memes. Some religious ideas may survive entirely because of their merit, independently of other memes. Some other ideas are successful only because they are compatible with other memes within a particular memeplex. It may be hypothesized that among the religious memes which have a high survival value are such ideas as the concept of life after death, or the statement that belief in God is a supreme virtue. Different religions can be seen as alternative memeplexes. This model of religion assumes that organized religions are not designed by individual people, but they evolve as alternative collections of memes. Genetic natural selection is too slow to account for the rapid evolution and divergence of religions. Memetic natural selection, on the other hand, can explain the incredible speed at which a new religious cult can start.

One striking example of this fact is provided by the so-called cargo cults of Pacific Melanesia and New Guinea. All these cults started recently as a result of the natives observing the shipping of cargo to the islands by the white people. The constant flow of goods was considered miraculous, and it gave rise to a number of rituals during which the natives tried to imitate the white people in order to bring more cargo to their islands. They built mockup runways, control towers, and even planes to lure the "gods" back to their islands. Several features of this case are worth noticing, including the amazing speed at which the cults sprang up quite independently from each other, and their striking resemblance to older, well-established religions, including Christianity.

6 HOW TO EXPLAIN MORALITY

Morality is often construed as an outgrowth of religious systems of beliefs. Some people find it difficult to imagine how we can be good without religion, or how moral principles can be justified without reference to a Divine Creator. But morality, like religion itself, can be traced back to some evolutionary adaptations. To begin with, it may seem that natural selection cannot explain the existence of the feelings of compassion, pity and altruism. The very notion of the selfish gene used by evolutionists seems to be in direct contradiction to human altruism. But we shouldn't confuse the selfishness of genes with the selfishness of individual organisms. Genes may be selfish in that their only "goal" is to promote their own survival and reproduction, but this goal need not be achieved by programming individual organisms to be selfish too. In some circumstances genes can ensure their selfish survival by making organisms behave altruistically.

Generally, four Darwinian reasons for altruistic behavior can be given. The first reason falls under the heading of kin altruism. Helping individuals who are related to us (our children in particular) clearly promotes our genes and increases their frequency in the gene pool. This is so thanks to the high probability that kin will share copies of the same genes. But altruism can be shown to total strangers too. The second type of evolutionary beneficial altruism is reciprocal altruism. Reciprocal altruism is the basis for the well-known biological phenomenon of symbiosis, as well as for trade and barter among humans. Symbiosis usually happens when members of different species profit from their mutual cooperation. A standard example of such cooperation is the symbiosis between bees and flowers: bees get nectar from flowers while flowers get pollinated. In humans reciprocal altruism creates the moral notion of obligation, and also identifies and ostracizes those who cheat by accepting favors and not repaying them.

Two further elements responsible for the sense of morality are reputation and, quite surprisingly, the need to assert dominance and superiority. Reputation is important as a survival value, because individuals with good reputation are more likely to receive favors from other individuals. As for the last factor, biologists have observed that some animals exhibit seemingly altruistic behavior towards other members of their species in order to assert their high position in the hierarchy. For instance, some birds feed their subordinates, but do not let them reciprocate, to show "who's boss". A similar behavior is observed in humans too. For example, rich people tend to be generous in order to show their superior social status.

But the four mentioned elements still don't explain a "Good Samaritan" attitude; that is the urge to help absolute strangers from outside one's group without expecting anything in return. This type of behavior can only be explained as a mistake, or a misfiring of a rule which was supposed to promote one of the four aforementioned goals. Mistakes of this kind often happen in the animal kingdom. Birds are programmed by evolution to feed their young in order to promote their own genes, but this rule misfires when a cuckoo chick takes place in their nest. Sex is the commonest method of reproduction in nature, and in order to ensure the continuation of the species evolution made us feel pleasure while having sex. But this feeling does not go away when we use contraception, even though the evolutionary purpose of sex cannot be satisfied in this case. Similarly, the feeling of pleasure that we have when helping our relatives is much the same as when we help others who are not related to us. That morality is a misfiring of the evolutionary mechanism of kin altruism or reciprocal altruism should obviously not be seen as degrading it or reducing its value.

If morality is a product of evolutionary adaptation, we should share some fundamental moral values and principles regardless of the differences in religion or culture.[12] Various studies seem to confirm that this is indeed the case. Mark

Hauser, a biologist from Harvard University, has done surveys in which he has asked the respondents to consider and solve difficult moral dilemmas. A typical situation used in the surveys involved a runaway streetcar threatening to kill a group of five people. The streetcar can be diverted onto a siding, but there is one person sitting there, unaware of the danger. Should we throw the switch in order to save the five people by letting the streetcar kill one innocent person? In a variant of this situation the five people can be saved but only by pushing an innocent bystander off an overhead bridge to stop the car. Yet another question was whether it is right to kill a healthy person in order to donate his organs to five dying patients. The answers received were similar regardless of whether the respondent was religious or an atheist. In the first case ninety percent of participants accepted the "collateral damage" to save the five people. But in the remaining cases the majority of respondents did not accept the proposed killings of innocent bystanders to save the others. This almost unanimous verdict can be explained by our strong moral opposition to using other people as means to achieve other goals.

If there is no God, does it make sense to be good? Those who answer this question in the negative seem to confuse morality with obedience, or even worse with fawning. If you are good only because you fear punishment or expect reward, this is hardly morality. While there are reasons to believe that many people would behave badly in the absence of policing, there is no evidence that atheists have lower morals in comparison with religious individuals. On the contrary, some studies show correlations between higher rates of religious belief and higher rates of crime. But believers often argue that without God there couldn't be any absolute standards of morality.[13] Without religion we wouldn't know what is right and what is wrong in the absolute sense. However, many philosophers disagree with that. For instance Immanuel Kant has developed an absolutist conception of morality (classified as deontology) which uses the concept of the categorical imperative. His view was essentially that morality is based on duty, and we should act in such a way that the principle behind our action could be turned into a universal law applicable to everyone in every circumstance. Another school in ethics is known as consequentialism. It holds that the moral value of an action depends only on its consequences. For utilitarians, such as Jeremy Bentham and John Stuart Mill, moral actions are such that bring the greatest amount of happiness to the greatest number of people. These are just a few examples of ethical systems which are naturalistic, that is independent of any religion.

7 THE MORAL VALUES OF THE BIBLE

Devout Christians believe that the Bible is the primary source of our moral values and principles. The main argument of this chapter aims to refute this conviction. The biblical text is full of stories which, when taken literally, flatly contradict our modern sense of morality, and thus it cannot be the root of our morals. And if we wanted to pick only some selected fragments and ignore or reinterpret the others, we would have to make this decision on the basis of something else that the Bible itself – presumably on the basis of our moral instincts. But this proves the point that Scripture alone is insufficient to form the basis of the knowledge of good and bad.

There are two ways in which the Bible can teach us about moral principles: either directly, by stating what we should and shouldn't do (as in the Ten Commandments), or indirectly, by way of example. Presumably we should be able to derive useful moral lessons from numerous stories in the Old and New Testaments, featuring both humans and God himself. The stories of the Old Testament are particularly intriguing, as they can hardly be reconciled with our basic moral feelings. Children's favorite story of Noah's Ark tells us about God's wrath which culminates in the decision to annihilate virtually all humanity (including innocent babies) for disobeying his commands. Noah's story became a reference point for appalling and callous sermons of radical preachers who blame natural disasters in which hundreds of thousands die on people's sins. In the similar biblical story of Sodom and Gomorrah two entire cities are wiped out, save one individual named Lot and his family. But even Lot's wife suffers a horrible fate for the seemingly minor offence of being curious, as she is turned into a pillar of salt when she looks back at the burning home town despite God's warnings. Clearly the God of the Old Testament is not to be trifled with.

Other shocking tales of the Old Testament include the story of Abraham, who received God's strict orders to sacrifice his son Isaac. Even though the whole situation turns out to be a test of Abraham's devotion, as an angel stays his hand at the last moment before Isaac's execution, still the willingness to kill one's own son is hardly seen as a moral virtue in modern culture (and Abraham's obedience to God is chillingly reminiscent of the excuse used frequently at the Nuremberg trial – "I was only following orders"). But in another, less-known story God is not so merciful. When a military leader named Jephthah promises God to sacrifice the first living thing that comes out of his house to meet him after his victorious battle, God does not relieve him of his duty even when the first person he meets at the house turns out to be his own daughter.

One of the most important figures of the Bible is unquestionably Moses, through whom God made a covenant with his people and gave them the Ten Commandments. So it may be interesting to note that Moses's list of achievements includes the order of the wholesale slaughter of all his fellow tribespeople who had committed the offence of worshipping the wrong god. In another episode Moses got furious with his soldiers who had spared the women and children of a vanquished Midianite city. He commanded them to go back and kill all the boys and all the non-virgin women. The fate of the Midianite virgins according to Moses's plans does not need much elaborating.

Regarding the direct commandments given by God in the Bible, it seems that the most important is the one which forbids worshipping other gods. The God of the Old Testament is a jealous one and, as we have seen, he punishes severely those who dare to turn their backs on him. The list of other offences punishable by death is long, and it includes cursing your parents, working on the Sabbath, adultery, and homosexuality. Modern apologists of Christianity often react to these examples by saying that they should not be taken out of their historical context. What was acceptable three thousand years ago does not have to agree with today's standards of justice and righteousness. This may be true, but it only goes to show that we can't learn our morals directly from the Bible. We need to interpret the stories of the Bible, but this requires that we already possess some independent criteria of what is moral and what is immoral.

The New Testament can be seen as an improvement over the bloody and frightening Old Testament. Nevertheless we can still find many controversial statements there. To begin with, it has to be admitted that Jesus's moral teachings are truly groundbreaking, as the Sermon of the Mount clearly attests. But his family values were lacking, as he was rather brusque in his relations with his mother and his family. The central theological doctrine of the New Testament, which is that Jesus died on the cross to atone for our sins, is bizarre in the extreme. Why would God see the death of his own son as necessary in order to forgive us our sins? And what sins are we talking about? The Christian conception of original sin which somehow passes from generation to generation is rather strange. Why should anybody bear moral responsibility for an act committed a long time ago by their forefathers? And even the nature of original sin itself raises many questions. Why was one relatively mild act of disobedience so grave that it marked all of humanity ever since? How would you punish your children for giving in to temptation and eating a piece of candy despite your orders? Would you throw them out of your house and never let them return, as God did with Adam and Eve?

Some people may still insist that the Bible contains universal and profound moral truths and principles, of which the "Love thy neighbor" exhortation is a prime example. But the truth is that this principle had a different meaning for the ancient Israelites than it has for the modern person. In fact, it most certainly meant to them "Love thy fellow Jew". It is characteristic that Jewish commentators of the Bible explicitly limit the applicability of the commandments to Israelites. Thus killing a gentile does not compromise the commandment "Thou shalt not kill". Sadly, this xenophobic attitude is not a thing of the past. In one study conducted by the Israeli psychologist George Tamarin, a group of Israeli schoolchildren were asked to give their moral evaluations of the biblical story of Joshua and his destruction of Jericho. Sixty-six percent of the children approved of the killing of all the inhabitants of Jericho by the Israelite soldiers, quoting reasons such as that God gave them permission, or that the vanquished people were of a different religion. And even those children who disapproved of the massacre gave peculiar reasons for their answers, such as that the city of Jericho should not be entered because it was impure, or that the soldiers should not have killed the animals or destroyed the property, because they might have been useful for the Israelites. The Bible can be seen as a blueprint for in-group morality, religious conflicts and religious intolerance of the sort we still witness in Northern Ireland or the Middle East.

In spite of what religious zealots want us to believe, our sense of what is right and what is wrong is largely independent of the holy texts.

Regardless of their differences, people are in a broad consensus with respect to fundamental moral principles, such as that causing unnecessary suffering is wrong, or that free speech should be protected. This consensus is, however, conspicuously different from the moral standards that were accepted in biblical times. Today slavery is unlawful, women and men are considered equal, and children are protected from abuse. Even some views of great nineteenth century figures, such as Thomas Huxley and Abraham Lincoln, would be considered highly inappropriate by today's standards. Although both men were staunch opponents of slavery, they nevertheless openly expressed the opinion that white men are superior to blacks, and that the two races should be separated. The changes in our standards of propriety illustrate what Dawkins calls the changing moral Zeitgeist. As the progression of the spirit of the times is clearly not caused by religion, it further supports the claim that morality is by and large independent from the belief in God.

The last considered strategy to defend the connection between morality and faith is based on the suggestion that non-believers are frequently immoral. An oft-cited example is that of Hitler and Stalin – two ruthless dictators responsible for the death of millions. Because they were atheists, it is suggested that atheism promotes evil. But this argument presupposes that Hitler and Stalin's evil deeds were directly and causally connected with their atheism, and this has not been proven. Generally, there is no evidence that atheism systematically influences people to do bad things. Moreover, the factual premise that both tyrants were non-believers can be questioned. While there is no doubt that Stalin was an atheist (although he received his education at an Orthodox seminary, and was prepared to be a priest), with Hitler the situation is far from clear. In some of his writings and speeches he portrays himself as a devout Christian, whereas in others he lashes out at Christianity. Hitler often spoke about a higher power ("Providence") which guided and protected him, and some even speculate that he was a member of a secret religious cult whose aim was to restore some of the ancient Germanic rituals and beliefs. The bottom line is, however, that individual atheists may do evil things, but they don't do them in the name of atheism. No war has been fought in the name of atheism, which is an absence of beliefs rather than a belief.[14]

8 THE DARKER SIDE OF RELIGION

Dawkins begins this chapter by addressing the charge that his own stance in the debate with radical theists is no less fundamentalist that that of his opponents. His response to this accusation is that people often confuse fundamentalism with passion. He is often passionate in discussions with his religious adversaries, but this is usually a result of his frustration at their stubborn refusal to accept rational argumentation. But Dawkins and other scientists are not fundamentalists, because they are ready to abandon their views in light of unfavorable evidence. Scientists adopt a critical attitude even towards their own theories, and they change their views if confronted with new facts and arguments. Dawkins uses an example of a respected professor of biology who was not afraid to admit publicly that he had been wrong after a discussion with a younger colleague. Such a situation is virtually unthinkable with religious fundamentalists. On the contrary, the exact opposite of a critical and open attitude is common in religious circles. One American geologist, who experienced a dramatic religious conversion, admitted in writing that even if all the evidence in the world spoke against creationism, he would still remain a creationist, because this is what God told him. Such an attitude can hardly be called scientific.

One particular reason why Dawkins seems to be so hostile towards religion is what he calls "the dark side of absolutism". Graphic examples of this phenomenon are provided by multiple cases of death sentences passed for violations of religious laws. Nowadays this problem affects mostly Islamic theocratic states, but in the not-so-distant past religious offences were punishable by law in the Western countries too.[15] In recent years a number of death sentences were handed out in Pakistan and Afghanistan for blasphemy and converting to Christianity. Homosexuality is also considered a crime in Muslim countries, and not so long ago it was penalized in Great Britain as well. The great mathematician and logician Alan Turing, whose work on cracking the German Enigma codes was invaluable for Britain, was prosecuted for homosexual behavior in 1954. He had been offered a choice between two years in prison and chemical castration, after which he chose a third option and took his own life.

Abortion is an issue which provokes strong reactions from religious fundamentalists. These reactions range from condemnation to intimidation, and in some cases even to murder. In 1994 a pastor from an organization calling themselves the Army of God shot dead a doctor from an abortion clinic and his bodyguard. The murderer then gave himself up to the police, and accepted the death penalty, portraying himself as a martyr. Apparently, for radical believers the life of a grown-up doctor is worth less than the lives of fetuses. But even those who oppose such violent actions as killing abortion doctors, nevertheless condemn abortions as equivalent to murder. But are they indeed? To begin with, Dawkins notes an apparent inconsistency in the views of some (but not all) defenders of life. Typically, anti-abortionists are also strong supporters of the death penalty (with the exception of Catholics). But this means that human life cannot have an absolute value for them. It is rather strange to argue that embryos shouldn't be killed because human life is sacred, and at the same time accept that it is morally admissible to execute adult, fully developed humans.[16]

The moral analysis of the abortion question can be done within the consequentialist ethic. We should take into account the issue of suffering (which, according to the utilitarians, is the opposite of happiness): how much suffering does an abortion cause? It may be argued that the embryo does not suffer, because its nervous system is not yet fully developed. On the other hand, the pregnant women may suffer if the abortion is not performed. But Dawkins admits that a consequentialist argument against abortion can be given as well. This is a 'slippery slope' argument, and it roughly states that because there is no clear borderline between fully developed children capable of suffering and unborn fetuses, it is best to err on the side of caution and not allow abortions, otherwise we may open the door to infanticide. A similar slippery slope argument can be given in the case of euthanasia: if we allowed mercy killing of a terminally ill patient, the next step would be euthanizing a 60-year old with a cold. Consequentialists may argue that admitting abortion and euthanasia can eventually create more suffering in the world because of the slippery slope effect.

However, Dawkins severely criticize yet another argument commonly used against abortion, known as the Beethoven argument. This argument, perpetuated on many Internet websites, asks proponents of abortion whether they would be willing to abort a child from a syphilitic father, whose other children suffered from various genetic disorders. After an inevitable positive answer, the arguer triumphantly announces "So you would have killed Beethoven". Dawkins first points out that this argument is based on a complete fabrication: in fact neither were Beethoven's siblings mentally or physically impaired, nor was his father a syphilitic. But these details are irrelevant, since the entire reasoning is fallacious anyway. Peter and Jean Medawar note in their book *The Life Science* that the argument could be equally well directed against sexual abstinence, since this would also have prevented a future Beethoven from being born. Dawkins adds to this a sarcastic remark that every time we pass up an opportunity to have a sexual intercourse we deprive a human soul of the gift of existence, which in the eyes of pro-life activists is tantamount to murdering a potential child.[17]

Extremisms are the dark side of religious absolutism. But it may be argued that even mild and moderate religious views help create an environment in which religious extremism can flourish. Cases of suicide bombers clearly show that these people's minds were primarily affected by religion and religious thinking, not extremism. If we agree that religious faith ought to be respected, we should also agree that bin Laden and suicide bombers deserve our respect. There are other ideologies besides religion which may lead to dangerous extremisms, such as nationalism or racism. However, religion is particularly dangerous, because by its very nature it discourages questioning. Some moderate believers explain that acts of terrorism, such as the World Trade Center attack or the London Underground bombing, are perversions of true faith. But this seems unconvincing, because faith doesn't have an objective justification and therefore we don't know what constitutes its perversion.

9 RELIGION AND CHILDREN

One important reason why religion deserves our scorn is the way it abuses children. This abuse may be physical, but much more dangerous is the mental type of abuse commonly seen in religious circles. Dawkins first reminds the reader that recently the Catholic Church has been under a fierce attack for alleged cases of sexual molestation. While obviously he is no big fan of the Catholic Church, Dawkins is convinced that the whole molestation issue has been blown out of proportion to the point of mass hysteria. He suggests that greedy lawyers and unscrupulous therapists might have contributed to the recent spate of child molestation lawsuits. However, a much more serious problem which has managed to slip under the radar of mass media is the everyday psychological abuse that most children suffer in silence, which is indoctrination by irrational and often horrifying religious ideas. Such ideas can leave permanent scars on the child's psyche no less deep than the scars from physical abuse. For instance, the vivid descriptions of hell and eternal torment that many religious teachers and priests expose their children to, often result in persistent nightmares and phobias experienced well into adulthood. Dawkins comments ironically that perhaps the frightening details of hell are a way to compensate for its high improbability.

The common practice of raising children in one faith selected by their parents without asking the children themselves may be seen as yet another form of abuse. Parents foist their beliefs on their children who are too young to make a decision regarding their faith. Instead, it would be much better to try to guess what the kids would choose if they were old enough to do so. Some open-minded parents decide not to teach their children what to think but how to think. They present the children with many options, leaving to them the final decision regarding their beliefs. But this is a rarity. Typically, Catholic parents raise their children as Catholics, Protestants as Protestants, and Jews as Jews. And if a child grows up and decides to change his or her faith, or worse become an atheist, this often results in ostracism in the family. Extreme examples of this kind of behavior can be found in strict religious communities, such as the Amish in the US.

The Amish people follow very rigorous religious rules which govern every detail of their lives, including the clothes they wear and the tools they use for work. In particular, they do not allow their children to attend public schools in order to protect them from what they see as the corrupting influence of modernity. When this issue was brought to court, the verdict was reached that the Amish parents should be allowed to choose whatever form of education they think is best for their children. While we may be sympathetic to this verdict as expressing our idea of religious tolerance, we may wonder if there is a limit to the parents' freedom of making choices on behalf of their children. Some argue that the children should have a say in this matter, and some go as far as to suggest that even if they expressed their consent to the parents' wishes, still we couldn't take this decision seriously unless the children had been thoroughly educated about all the available alternatives.

Some liberals tend to defend the right of people like the Amish to make even the most absurd decisions regarding the upbringing of their children from the position of multiculturalism or diversity. According to this stance, communities such as that of the Amish are worth protecting in order to preserve the richness and diversity of cultures on Earth. But this approach can lead to ludicrous consequences. Ancient Incas used to make ritual sacrifices of their children to gods. Are the proponents of multiculturalism ready to accept this practice out of respect for the Inca culture and tradition? Or perhaps we should use yet another fashionable notion of cultural and moral relativism to argue that what seems to us a cruel, cold-blooded murder of an innocent child can be equally well treated as a sacred, holy ritual for the benefit of the community, and that there is no telling which perspective is better?

We are so used to the idea that children who are born into a family with particular religious beliefs will subscribe to the same beliefs, that we use the labels "Christian child", "Muslim child" with no qualms. But Dawkins decries this apparently innocent practice. We should keep in mind that the decision to accept some particular religious beliefs is not made by the children but by their parents. It would be much better to say "a child of Christian parents" than "a Christian child", since the latter label wrongly suggests that the child voluntarily agreed to be a member of the Christian community. Such a terminology would also be better for the child herself, for it would draw her attention to the fact that ultimately it should be her decision and not somebody else's (not even her parents) to follow a particular religion.

Dawkins is clearly in favor of secularist public education which should teach children objective, scientific facts and principles according to our best scientific theories. He strongly condemns attempts to use public funds to support religious schools which teach creationist alternatives to the scientifically accepted evolutionary theory. However, Dawkins insists that biblical studies should be part of national curricula as an element of cultural literacy. He laments the deplorable ignorance of the Bible and its role in art and literature which is common even among religious people. Some polls show for instance that a significant percentage of Catholics and Protestants in America have problems with identifying who Moses was, or who gave the Sermon on the Mount. People are also ignorant of the fact that so many phrases and proverbs commonly used today, such as "the apple of his eye" or "physician heal thyself", are taken directly from the Bible. There is nothing wrong with learning about the Bible, or taking part in religious rituals out of loyalty to our traditions, but we don't need to buy into the supernatural beliefs which went along with these traditions.[18]

10 CONSOLATION AND COMFORT

The last line of defense for the apologists of religion is an argument pointing out that the belief in God offers comfort and consolation. It is well known that many people find solace in religion especially in times of hardship, when they are confronted with personal tragedies such as death in the family or an illness. Belief in God also alleviates our fear of dying by giving us a perspective of an afterlife. But Dawkins notes first that even if it were proven that religion is essential to our emotional well-being, this would not show that it is true. At best this could be an argument for the desirability of convincing oneself that God exists. Using the terminology introduced by the philosopher Daniel Dennett, we can distinguish between belief in God and belief in belief. Only the latter belief can be possibly supported by the argument from consolation. However, it is by no means obvious that only believers can find comfort and happiness in their life. There are many atheists who lead a happy and fulfilled life without holding any beliefs in the supernatural.

In order to understand better how a non-believer can find emotional comfort without God, let us distinguish two types of consolation. First, there may be direct physical consolation, involving things such as hugging or whispering reassuring words. Another type of consolation happens when we realize that there are certain facts which can put our grief and suffering in a new perspective or make them easier to bear. For instance, the thought that her husband died while saving someone's life may be a consolation for a bereaved wife. How effective in these two types of consoling is religion in comparison to science? It may be claimed that God is capable of physical consolation (at least in human imagination), but medicine can also provide physical comfort to people in distress. But the most common type of consolation delivered by religion is of the second, indirect kind. A person experiencing a tragic event may explain this to herself by saying that it is part of God's inscrutable plan which has a higher, albeit hidden from us, purpose. The fear of dying can be alleviated by the thought that we have an immortal soul. Incidentally, in spite of the fact that approximately 95 percent of Americans admit to believing in some form of afterlife, this belief does not seem to be strong enough to change our reaction to the death of others and to our own future death. Why don't devout Christians revel at the news of the death of their relatives? Shouldn't they feel happy for them that they have finally achieved eternal bliss in heaven? Seen from this perspective, death should be an occasion to celebration, not grief.

It may be claimed that atheists can find solace in the naturalistic worldview as well as the believers can find it in religion. Many people observe that being dead is essentially the same as being unborn. For billions of years before our birth we were non-existent. Why, then, should we fear returning to this state? And if what we fear is the pain and suffering of the process of dying, then one simple answer to this is painless euthanasia or assisted suicide. Another consoling thought available to the atheist is that everyone should be already familiar with death to a certain extent. When we grow older, we go through a process which gradually and irreversibly alters our psyche. Some of our memories fade away, and our earlier habits and preferences are replaced by new ones. Our earlier selves are in a sense no longer present, as if they have already died. But ultimately the difference between the consolations offered by science and by religion is that the latter is based on a *non sequitur*. The fact that we need God to console and comfort us does not in the least make his existence more probable. It is childish to imagine that the world will bend to our wishes. Dawkins compares the emotional comfort that we derive from our belief in God to children's game of imaginary friends. Many children go through a period when they take comfort in imagining that they have a playmate who can keep them company when everybody else in the family is busy. But all children outgrow their imaginary friends sooner or later. Mayn't it be the case that our belief in God is just a protracted game with an imaginary friend which we don't want to grow out of?

Abandoning the belief in God can leave a gap in the life of many people. Different people will try to fill this gap in different ways. Dawkins's personal way of filling it is with the help of science. He marvels at how science manages to expand our horizons and open our eyes to the previously unknown wonders of the universe. By nature our senses are severely limited in their abilities to create an adequate picture of the world surrounding us. Our eyes can detect only a tiny fraction of the existing spectrum of electromagnetic radiation. Our senses of smell and hearing are equally restricted. We are equipped to perceive only midsize objects ranging from a tenth of a millimeter to a couple of kilometers. And yet science gives as a way to overcome these serious limitations, allowing us to peer behind the veil of ignorance.

But to do that we often need to abandon our common sense. Our senses tell us that things around us are hard and impenetrable, but physics teaches us that they are mostly made up of empty space and tiny swirling atoms. Our way of perceiving the world has been shaped by millions of years of evolution, but this is by no means the only way possible. Other creatures have their own ways of obtaining and processing data about their surroundings. Bats register ultrasounds through echolocation to navigate in the darkness. Dogs can detect trace amounts of chemicals using their acute sense of smell. Only science can enable us to imagine what the world may look like to other creatures. It seems that there is no limit to what science can achieve in the future.

11 HIGHLIGHTS

There is no reason why religions and religious beliefs should be treated with special respect not granted to other types of beliefs. Religious views should not be immune from criticism only because such criticism may be considered offensive by the believers.

The God Hypothesis asserts the existence of a supernatural, superhuman intelligent being who created the universe and constantly maintains and supervises it.

Agnostics assign equal probabilities to the God Hypothesis and its negation. But the fact that we don't have a conclusive proof that the God Hypothesis is false does not imply that we should be completely agnostic with respect to it. The burden of proof principle states that unless the proponents of a given existential hypothesis give positive arguments for its truth, this hypothesis should be assumed false pending further arguments.

The popular view that science and religion are separated areas of knowledge which can't be compared with one another flies in the face of the fact that religion makes a lot of claims about the world, such as the claims about miraculous occurrences, which can be scientifically tested.

Philosophical arguments in support of God's existence, which have been formulated throughout history, are woefully inadequate. Arguments from authority and from individual religious experiences are equally unconvincing.

Theists use the God hypothesis to explain the unlikely occurrence of irreducibly complex systems. This strategy fails, because the existence of God is even more improbable than the events which it is supposed to explain.

The main error committed by creationists is the assumption that complex organisms can only arise either by chance or by design. The theory of evolution offers a third solution, according to which natural selection works through a series of gradual improvements which accumulate over time. The complexity of organisms created in that way is high, but it is by no means irreducible, as we can clearly identify transitional forms and earlier, less developed variants of the currently existing biological structures.

It is a challenge to explain the ubiquity of religion in terms of natural selection. Most probably religious beliefs and rituals are side effects of some adaptations useful for survival. Several hypotheses regarding what these adaptations may be proposed. One suggestion is that the root of religion lies in the unconditional obedience and trust that children display toward their parents. Another possibility is that the beneficial adaptation responsible for religion is instinctive dualism and teleology, or the phenomenon of romantic love.

The development and spreading of various religious cults can be best explained in terms of the memetic theory. Memes are units of cultural inheritance which replicate in an analogous way to genes.

Morality can be given a Darwinian explanation too. Most probably, morality is a result of four main adaptations: kin altruism, reciprocal altruism, spreading reputation, and dominance.

Morality can also be derived from some fundamental philosophical principles independently from any religious system of beliefs. Two dominating schools in moral philosophy are deontology (represented by Immanuel Kant) and consequentialism (supported by Jeremy Bentham and John Stuart Mill).

In spite of common misperception, the Bible can hardly be seen as the source of our morals, since numerous biblical stories contradict our modern sense of good and bad. Interpretations of the Bible offered by modern religions require an independent point of reference for our morals.

Fundamentalism of religious believers is shown in their inability to change their views even when confronted with unquestionable evidence. In contrast to that, scientists are always ready to abandon their theories if they are disconfirmed by experience.

Religious fanaticism spawns violence and intolerance. This can be confirmed by examples of numerous military conflicts throughout the world, as well as by the abuse of religious laws in theocratic states.

The radical anti-abortion stance of religious fundamentalists cannot be supported by rational arguments. Utilitarian ethics does not justify equating abortion with murder, and typical arguments offered by anti-abortionists (such as the Beethoven argument) are fallacious.

The practice of raising children in the faith of their parents can be argued to be a form of their mental abuse. The choice of a particular religion is made for the children without their consent and without them fully understanding all the alternatives.

Public education should include biblical and religious studies as part of cultural literacy.

While religious beliefs can offer emotional comfort and consolation, this does not prove that they are true. Abandoning the concept of God can leave a gap in the lives of many people, but this gap can be filled in many different ways, for instance by science.

NOTES FROM CURIOUS READER

[1]Later in the chapter Dawkins explains the difference between supernatural and superhuman as follows: superhuman intelligent beings (for instance hypothetical aliens) are still products of a natural evolution from less to more complex structures, whereas supernatural entities owe their existence to no natural processes.

[2]Historians argue that the cult of Virgin Mary in early Christianity was closely modeled on pagan cults of various female deities, for instance of the Egyptian goddess Isis, who was very popular in ancient Rome at the beginning of the first millennium.

[3]Philosophers associated with the influential twentieth century movement called logical positivism believed that statements for which it is in

principle impossible to decide whether they are true or false should be treated as meaningless. For them the God Hypothesis would belong to the category of meaningless expressions, neither true nor false.

[4] It seems that in this case it is more appropriate to be an agnostic of the TAP type rather than the PAP type. That is, the existence of a teapot in the solar system could in principle be proved if we had sufficiently advanced technology at our disposal. However, it is easy to think of a different example in which PAP would be applicable as well. For instance, we may consider the hypothesis stating that there are invisible fairies around us which could under no circumstances be observed or detected in any way.

[5] The caveat "without additional reasons to believe that such a teapot should exist" is important here. Theists would obviously reply that they do have important reasons to believe in God's existence. Some of these reasons will be presented and criticized in the next chapter.

[6] The burden of proof principle may be slightly generalized. Each time we consider an existential hypothesis (a hypothesis stating that something exists), the proponents of the hypothesis have the responsibility to give their reasons for believing that it is true. The lack of evidence that the hypothesis is false does not constitute a positive argument for its

truth. This applies to all cases of existential statements, whether involving atoms, genes, Higgs bosons, or aliens from outer space.

[7] All the five arguments given by St Thomas are full of logical gaps not mentioned by Dawkins. To list only a few: from the fact that each causal chain of events has to have an initial element not caused by anything it does not follow that there is one cause of everything (each chain may have its own "ultimate" cause). Similarly, the argument from degree can at best establish that for each quality there is an entity possessing it in the highest degree, but it falls short of proving that there is exactly one entity possessing all qualities in the highest degree. Actually, this is even logically impossible, since some of these qualities may be mutually inconsistent.

[8] Most philosophers would disagree with this brief characterization of Hume's and Kant's criticism of Anselm's proof. Kant's critique is usually interpreted as questioning the hidden premise of the argument that existence is a property which some objects may lack. According to Kant's view, if we say for instance that Zeus doesn't exist, we don't mean by that that Zeus lacks the property of existence, but rather that simply there is no Zeus at all (no object in the universe possesses all the properties attributed to Zeus). This detail turns out to be crucial for the validity of the ontological argument, because Anselm argues that God who

does not exist would be a less perfect being than an existing God. But if there is no non-existent God, the entire argument collapses under its own weight.

[9]More precisely, Bayes's theorem states that the probability of a hypothesis H being true given a piece of evidence e is equal to the likelihood that e obtains given that H is true times our initial estimation of the likelihood of H, divided by the probability of e regardless of any assumption. One crucial feature of this theorem is that it can be applied over and over again when new evidence emerges. To do that we have to take the estimation of the probability of H given the last piece of evidence and insert this value in place of the initial likelihood of H in the formula.

[10]One likely response to this argument from the theists is that God's existence does not need any explanation (it is "self-explanatory"). After all, even scientists admit that the "why" questions cannot go forever – they must stop somewhere. But the theists fail to give a convincing reason why we can't stop our quest for explanation at the level of the material world.

[11]Some may complain that the anthropic principle not so much explains why life occurred on Earth as simply dodges the question. Children often pester their parents with the question "Why was I born?". But the answer "Because if you hadn't been born

you wouldn't be able to ask this question" seems to be just a mild version of "Shut up and eat your porridge".

[12]On the other hand, given the assumption that morality is a product of evolution, we should also observe variations in accepted moral values between cultures which grow up in different environmental conditions. This fact is confirmed by numerous anthropological studies. Generally, human societies that live in severe environmental conditions often develop harsh rules of conduct which may seem deeply immoral from our perspective. Some tribes for instance don't care for the older members of the community who can't take care of themselves, often letting them die of starvation or exposure.

[13]Morality based on God's commands is open to the following problem, which has been already noted by the Greek philosopher Plato in his dialogue "Eutyphro" (and, hence, is often called the Eutyphro problem): is a given action good because it is accepted by God, or does God accept it because it is good? If the first is the case, then morality is reduced to following orders which may or may not agree with our inner sense of goodness. But if we insist that God always prefers things that are intrinsically morally good, this means that there has to be a standard of morality independent of God's preferences.

[14]This statement can be questioned on the basis of historical evidence. It is surprising that Dawkins almost completely ignores the example of communism and its official atheist ideology. His remarks about Stalin are scanty, and they seem to suggest that atheism was just his private opinion having nothing to do with politics. In fact, hostility toward organized religion was a hallmark of all communist movements. During the Russian revolution of 1917 and the ensuing civil war the Bolsheviks were particularly ruthless in their attacks on the Russian Orthodox Church – they executed much of the clergy and destroyed or appropriated the Church property. Atheism was an official doctrine having an almost religious status in the Soviet Union and its satellite countries.

[15]But we shouldn't forget that people have also been persecuted for following their religious beliefs in secular countries, such as the former Soviet Union or China. It seems that the problem lies not in religion or atheism, but rather in the dictatorial character of some states which intrude into the private lives of their citizens.

[16]However, this argument can be easily turned around. Religious conservatives often accuse liberals of a similar inconsistency by pointing out that they condemn executions of convicted criminals who had been given a fair trial in a court

of law, and yet accept killing innocent babies on the basis of a single person's decision which cannot be even appealed.

[17]It may be argued that Dawkins does not do justice to all aspects of the complex and multifaceted problem of abortion. To begin with, his argument for abortion from the lack of suffering can raise legitimate questions. If suffering is the only thing that has moral consequences, would it be ethical to kill someone after giving him an anesthetic so that he wouldn't feel any pain or suffer from any fear? It may be replied that in this case the immoral character of the killing comes from the fact that we are robbing this person of his potential future. But why can't we apply the same argument to an unborn child? Dawkins ridicules the Beethoven argument by extending the argument against abortion to the case of a refusal of having sex. But there is an important difference between the two cases. Abortion deprives the *actual* fetus of a *potential* future, whereas the decision of not having sex merely fails to actualize a *potential* fetus. Other related arguments used by Dawkins similarly miss the point. For instance, commenting on the fact that during in vitro fertilization procedures many embryos are lost, Dawkins remarks that natural pregnancies are also frequently terminated. This argument is only marginally better than a murderer's excuse that the victim would die anyway of natural causes.

[18] It is not clear what Dawkins's suggested solution to the problem of the religious indoctrination of children should look like. Some of his remarks may be interpreted as advocating the state's intervention in the family's affairs similar to the interventions made in the cases of physical child abuse. But such a medicine would be much worse than the disease. It would require constant invigilation of the citizens, and would most probably violate their fundamental rights to privacy and freedom of beliefs. It seems that the right of the parents to raise their children in any way they see appropriate is an important civil right which can be suspended only in extreme cases of child abuse. For someone like Dawkins, who is seriously concerned about the possible side effects of religious indoctrination, the only available strategy is to educate the parents about the dangers of rigorous religious upbringing.

Also available from Curious Reader:

Good Habits, Bad Habits. A Critical Discussion of Charles Duhigg's "The Power of Habit"

Sweet Dreams. A Concise Summary of David K. Randall's "Dreamland: An Adventure in the Strange Science of Sleep"

Printed in Great Britain
by Amazon